EVERYDAY LIFE IN

VIKING TIMES

HAZEL MARY MARTELL

SEA-TO-SEA

Mankato Collingwood London

This edition first published in 2006 by
Sea-to-Sea Publications
1980 Lookout Drive
North Mankato
Minnesota 56003

Printed in China

Library of Congress Cataloging-in-Publication Data:

Martell, Hazel
    Everyday life in Viking Times/by Hazel Mary Martell.
        p. cm. — (Clues to the past)
    Originally published: New York: Franklin Watts, c1994.
    Includes index.
    ISBN 1-932889-80-9
    1. Vikings—Social life and customs—Juvenile literature. 2. Northmen—Social life and
    customs—Juvenile literature. 3. Social history—Medieval, 500-1500—Juvenile literature. I.
    Title. II. Series.

    DL65.M358 2005
    948'.022—dc22

                                                                    2004063720

9 8 7 6 5 4 3 2

Published by arrangement with the Watts Publishing Group Ltd, London

Editor: Sarah Ridley
Designer: Alan Cassedy
Illustrator: Tony Smith
Picture researcher: Joanne King

Photographs: Ancient Art and Architecture
Collection (L Eilison) 7bl, (Ronald Sheridan) 22, 28;
courtesy of the Trustees of the
British Museum, London (K107623) 8;
C M Dixon 30; Werner Forman Archive 7tl,
(British Museum, London) 6br,
(Viking Ship Museum, Bygdoy) 20,
(University Museum of National Antiquities,
Uppsala, Sweden) 24; Michael Holford front cover bl, 14, 26;
© Mats Wibe Lund 10; © University Museum
of National Antiquities, Oslo, Norway front cover br, 12t, 16;
York Archaeological Trust 4, 6t, 6bl, 7cr, 7br, 12b, 18.

CONTENTS

4 WHO WERE THE VIKINGS?

The Vikings lived over one thousand years ago in the lands we now call Denmark, Norway, and Sweden. They were mainly farmers and shipbuilders. However, their land was not very good for farming. Norway was very hilly, Sweden was covered in forests, and Denmark had a lot of sandy heathland. This meant that when the population increased, there was not enough land for everyone.

So, by the end of the eighth century, some Vikings began to look for other ways to make a living. At first they raided towns and monasteries in other parts of northwestern Europe. They stole the treasures and took the people as slaves. Some individuals at the time wrote down accounts of these raids, which were passed down through time.

For a long time, this was all that was known about the Vikings. More recently, however, archaeologists have been able to tell us more about the Vikings and their lives. We know that they traveled overseas to settle and trade, as well as to go raiding. They were skilled at metalwork, as well as carving in stone and wood. They also told great stories, which we can still read today.

This stone cross from Middleton on the Wolds, Yorkshire, shows a Viking warrior with some of his weapons. It was carved in the tenth century.

SOME IMPORTANT DATES IN VIKING TIMES

793 The Viking Age starts when Viking raiders attack Lindisfarne, off the northeastern coast of England.

840 Viking traders from Sweden reach Constantinople, which they call Miklagard, meaning "great city."

874 Vikings from Norway begin to settle in Iceland.

886 England is divided and the Vikings settle in the part known as the Danelaw.

GREENLAND

Western settlement

Eastern settlement

ICELAND

NEWFOUNDLAND

FAROES

SHETLANDS

ORKNEYS

SCOTLAND

IRELAND

ENGLAND

Normandy

NORWAY

SWEDEN

DENMARK

RUSSIA

Staraya Ladoga

Novgorod

Kiev

Istanbul

THE VIKING WORLD

The design of their ships let the Vikings sail farther than any other Europeans at that time. As the map shows, they settled in Scotland, Ireland, England, Iceland, Greenland, and Normandy. Some reached North America, while others sailed down the rivers of Russia to the Black Sea and Constantinople.

MAP KEY

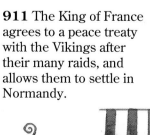

Viking homelands

Viking settlements

911 The King of France agrees to a peace treaty with the Vikings after their many raids, and allows them to settle in Normandy.

982 Eirik the Red discovers Greenland. After five years, Vikings from Iceland begin to settle there.

1003 Leif Eiriksson sails from Greenland to North America and explores Vinland.

1066 William, Duke of Normandy, invades England. The Viking Age soon comes to an end.

HOW DO WE KNOW ABOUT THE VIKINGS?

A lot of our clues to life in Viking times come from evidence discovered by archaeologists. By carefully excavating artifacts and other evidence from a site and studying them scientifically, archaeologists can build up a picture of how people lived in that place at a certain time in the past.

All the evidence that is found has to be weighed up carefully to take into account the objects that will probably have perished over time because of what they are made of. The examples shown on this page give a selection of some of the surviving objects from Viking times.

The archaeological site at Coppergate, York. It has given us a wealth of information about Viking life and is one of the most important sites outside Scandinavia.

LEATHER AND WOOD

Objects made from leather and wood usually rot away quickly in the soil. However, if the soil is waterlogged this helps to preserve items, such as shoes and boots, which would normally have perished. Whole wooden bowls have even been found.

COINS

Gold and silver coins have been found on many Viking sites. By studying where they were made, archaeologists can learn a great deal about where the Vikings traveled and who they traded with. These gold coins from England were found in Denmark. A coin from Samarkand in Asia was found on the Coppergate site in York, England.

WOOD CARVINGS

From the few examples which have survived, we know that the Vikings were skilled wood carvers. Some of the best examples of their craft are found on panels, like these from the church at Urnes in Norway. They are from the end of the Viking age and show the tree of life.

EVIDENCE IN THE LANDSCAPE

Evidence for some Viking burials can still be seen today. These stones, which are set out in the shape of a ship, mark a Viking grave at Ballandorae in the Isle of Man.

BONE AND ANTLER

One of the most common finds on Viking sites is the bone comb, like this one made from deer antlers. Bone was shaped into buckles for belts and also used for spindle whorls, to give weight and spin.

SEEDS

As well as looking for objects made by people, archaeologists also look for clues to what the environment was like in the past. One way they can do this is by sieving samples of soil and removing the remains of seeds, animal bones, and insects. These can then be studied under a microscope to find out what had lived on the site at a certain time. Seeds and animal bones also give clues to what people ate.

A rchaeological evidence shows that Viking tools were made from iron and wood. The scythe shown here was used to cut the grass in the meadows at haymaking time. Its blade has survived but its wooden handle has rotted away.

Other Viking tools have been found, including spades, forks, axes, knives, and sickles. Many of them are similar in shape to the tools of today.

Knife

Scythe

VIKING FARMERS

Most Vikings spent at least some of their time farming. They grew enough food to feed themselves and their families. In the north they grew oats, barley, and rye, but further south wheat could be grown, too. The Vikings also grew vegetables, such as onions and peas, and fruit, such as apples and cherries.

Many Vikings also kept cows, sheep, goats, pigs, and hens. The cows gave them leather, as well as meat and milk. Wool from the sheep was woven into cloth, and feathers from the hens were used to stuff pillows and mattresses.

Fishing was important to farmers who lived near rivers or fjords. Any fish that they did not eat at once was smoked, dried, or salted and eaten later.

THE CROPS
Grain crops at this time did not produce as many seeds as they do today. This was because the Vikings had no fertilizers apart from manure. The crops were also more likely to be attacked by pests, as there were no pesticides.

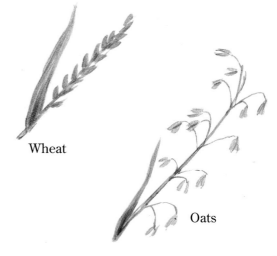

Barley

Rye

Wheat

Oats

The Vikings grew grain crops in the fields around their farms. They grew onions, peas, and cabbages in their gardens, where they also kept their geese, chickens, and pigs.

THE FARMING YEAR

In spring, the fields were plowed and seeds were sown. Then the hayfields were spread with manure to make the grass grow well. In Norway, the cattle and sheep were taken to summer mountain pastures until after the harvest. Elsewhere, animals grazed around the farmstead. Strong ones were kept over the winter, but weak ones were killed as there was not enough food for all of them.

THE ANIMALS
Farm animals in Viking times were smaller and skinnier than they are today. The pigs were darker and more hairy, while the sheep and cattle had longer horns.

VIKING HOMES

This picture shows a reconstruction of a farmhouse at Stöng in Iceland. The original buildings were buried in a volcanic eruption. When archaeologists excavated the site in 1939, they found enough evidence buried under the ash to make this full-size reconstruction. This is probably the best evidence we have for a Viking-type farmhouse, as most of them were built on sites which are still in use today.

THE LONGHOUSE

Viking houses are often called longhouses. This is because they were usually oblong in shape. The main building was up to 100 ft (30 m) long, but other buildings might be added on.

In the Viking homelands there were plenty of trees, so the walls of the houses were built of wood and the roofs were thatched with straw or reeds. Where there were not many trees, however, the walls were built from slabs of turf on a stone base with roofs made from thatch or turf. Sometimes the grass in the turf was allowed to keep on growing on the roof as this helped to keep the house warm.

Another method of house building was wattle and daub. Upright posts were woven together with twigs and then daubed with thick mud to keep out the draft.

Wood

BUILDING MATERIALS
The building materials used by the Vikings varied from area to area, depending on availability. Wattle and daub, wood, turf, straw, and stones were all used.

Wattle

Straw

Stones

Turf

Viking children were kept busy feeding the chickens and pigs, pulling up weeds, and chasing birds off growing crops.

DRYING FISH

In the far north, the Vikings preserved some of their fish by drying it. To do this, they first cleaned the fish. Then they slit each one along the belly and flattened it out. Finally, each fish was hung over a wooden rack and left out to dry in the sun.

AROUND THE HOUSE

In fine weather, the Vikings did a lot of work outside their houses. They looked after their vegetable gardens and also did any repairs that were needed on the house. If they had washed any clothes, they dried them in the open air. Wood was chopped and stacked ready to burn on the fire in winter. Another everyday job was fetching water from the well or a nearby stream for cooking, drinking, and washing. The Vikings also did messy jobs outside. These included tanning animal skins to make them into leather.

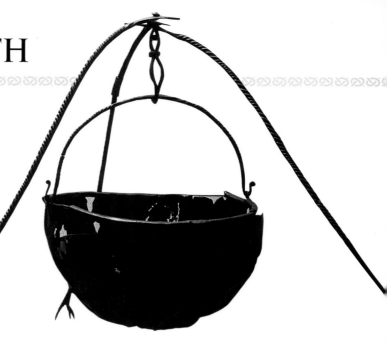

I ron caldrons were found in many Viking homes. The metal they were made from was quite thin. This meant that the caldron had to be suspended from a tripod over the fire to stop the flames from touching the bottom and burning a hole through it. Caldrons were used for heating water as well as for cooking food. Many Vikings made items like this themselves in a small smithy on their farm.

HOME LIFE

Many Viking homes had only one room and the hearth was at the center of it. To stop the flames from spreading out and setting the house on fire, the hearth was usually surrounded by stones or pieces of wood.

The flames from the fire gave heat and helped to give light in the windowless room, although there were lamps as well. This meant that all household activities took place as near to the fire as possible. These included preparing food and cooking it, spinning wool and weaving cloth, making clothes, sleeping, and eating.

It could be quite crowded inside the house as three generations of the same family might live together. As well as children, parents, and grandparents, the family often also included unmarried aunts and uncles.

Although family ties were important to the Vikings, sons were sometimes sent to live with foster parents. The foster family then became as important as the real family and could rely on the foster son's support in times of trouble.

MYSTERY
O B J E C T

This object was found during the excavation at Coppergate in York, England. It is made from iron and is $3^3/_8$ in (8·6 cm) long. It has been taken apart for this picture, but when it is in use the pieces all fit together. What do you think it is? Clue: it helped the Vikings to keep their belongings safe. You will find the answer on page 32.

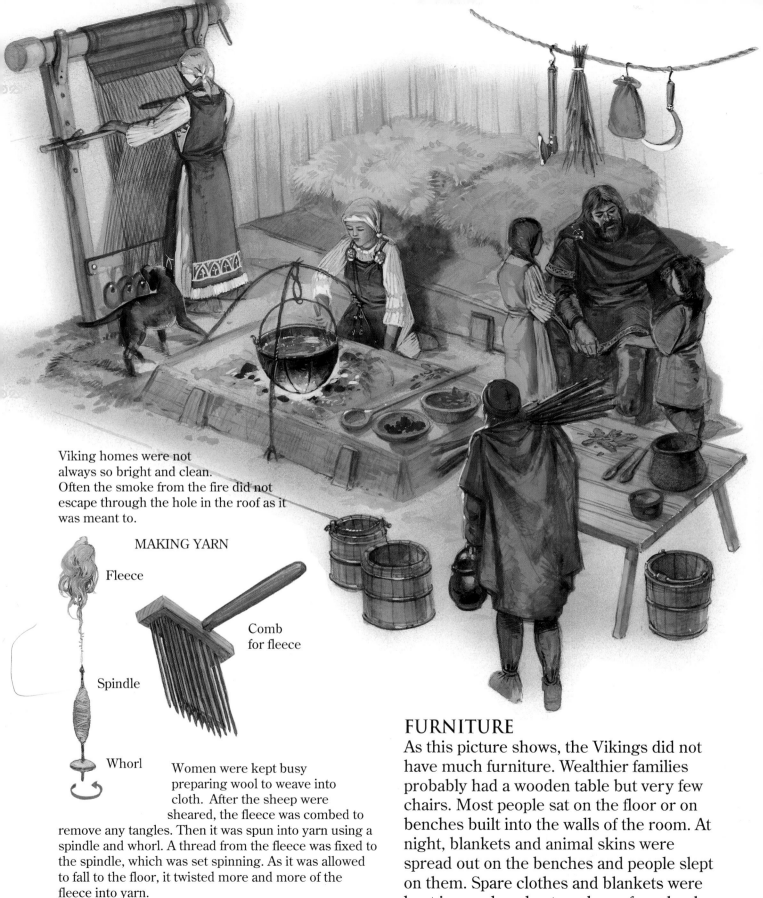

Viking homes were not always so bright and clean. Often the smoke from the fire did not escape through the hole in the roof as it was meant to.

MAKING YARN

Fleece

Comb for fleece

Spindle

Whorl

Women were kept busy preparing wool to weave into cloth. After the sheep were sheared, the fleece was combed to remove any tangles. Then it was spun into yarn using a spindle and whorl. A thread from the fleece was fixed to the spindle, which was set spinning. As it was allowed to fall to the floor, it twisted more and more of the fleece into yarn.

FURNITURE

As this picture shows, the Vikings did not have much furniture. Wealthier families probably had a wooden table but very few chairs. Most people sat on the floor or on benches built into the walls of the room. At night, blankets and animal skins were spread out on the benches and people slept on them. Spare clothes and blankets were kept in wooden chests or hung from hooks on the walls.

The Vikings knew how to make pottery, but they did not often use it for cups and plates. Instead, they used it for storage jars like these. The pots would be used to contain foodstuffs, such as flour, hazelnuts, and buttermilk. Good-quality pots were often taken to be sold in markets a long way from where they were made.

THE VIKING DIET

The Vikings ate two main meals each day. They had the first one at about eight o'clock in the morning. The second one was eaten at about seven o'clock in the evening.

By studying bones and seeds found on Viking sites, archaeologists can tell us a lot about what the Vikings ate. As well as meat from the pigs, sheep, and cattle they kept on their farms, the Vikings ate meat from wild animals, such as boar and deer, which they hunted. They ate eggs from hens, geese, and ducks. They also picked wild berries and plants, including raspberries and strawberries, cress, mustard, and hazelnuts.

Most Vikings drank beer or buttermilk with their meals, but on special occasions they had wine or mead, which was made from honey.

DAIRY PRODUCE

Dairy produce was an important part of the Vikings' daily diet. They drank a lot of milk as well as buttermilk. This was the thin milk that was left after the cream had been removed to be made into butter. Soft cheese was made by heating the milk until it separated into solid parts, called curds, and a watery liquid, called whey. Cheese was made from the curds, using a cheese strainer, while the whey was sometimes used to preserve other food.

Dairy cow

Cheese strainer

Viking women spent a lot of their time baking bread and cooking meat, fish, and vegetables.

MAKING BREAD
Bread was usually made from barley, and rye was used sometimes. The grains were ground into flour in a quern.

The quern was made from two circular stones, placed one on top of the other. The grain went on the bottom one and was ground up as the top one was rotated on it.

The bread dough was then mixed and kneaded in a wooden trough by the fire. It was shaped into loaves and baked on a flat stone slab, or griddle, placed over the fire.

PREPARING MEAT
Meat was usually cut up and cooked slowly in a caldron over the fire. This helped to make it tender, especially if it had been dried or salted for any length of time. Vegetables and herbs were added to the stew to give it more flavor. Sometimes joints of pork or ham were boiled in water and then sliced up to be eaten. Meat could also be roasted on a spit over the fire or baked in a pit filled with embers and covered over with soil.

This jewelry is from a woman's grave in Sweden. She needed the brooches to fasten her clothes, as there were no zippers or buttons then. She wore one of the oval brooches on each side of her chest to fasten the straps of her tunic. A third brooch was often worn on the shoulder, with a chain hanging from it to hold items such as a comb or bunch of keys, as Viking clothes had no pockets.

CLOTHES

The Vikings mainly dressed for comfort, although styles did change in some places, especially for women. Men usually wore tight-fitting trousers made from woolen cloth. They also wore a long-sleeved tunic. This sometimes reached as far as their knees, but was usually shorter. It had a belt at the waist. The tunic sometimes also had an open neck. One Viking woman is said to have divorced her husband for showing too much bare chest under his tunic! In winter, both men and women wore long cloaks that fastened on the shoulder with a pin or brooch.

In Scandinavia, women wore a long-sleeved shift dress made from linen, with a woolen tunic over the top. In England, women turned to just wearing a long shift. All married women covered their hair with a scarf. Children wore clothes similar to those of their parents, but young girls usually kept their heads uncovered, unless the weather was very cold.

MYSTERY OBJECT

This item was found in a Viking woman's grave. It is quite large and is made from whalebone. It was found with a smaller, smooth glass object. What do you think they were both used for? You will find the answer on page 32.

Here you can see how Viking men, women, and children relied on brooches to keep their clothes fastened.

Both men and women wore flat-heeled leather shoes or boots that fastened around the ankle with a leather thong.

HOW DO WE KNOW?

Cloth rots quickly in the ground so no complete Viking outfit has been found. However, we know what clothes were like from stone carvings and written descriptions.

We also know about the color of the cloth as archaeologists have analyzed the dyes used in the small scraps of cloth they have found. They know that the Vikings used vegetable dyes, such as woad, madder, and weld. These gave blue, red, and yellow dyes. More colors, such as green, purple, and orange, were made by mixing them.

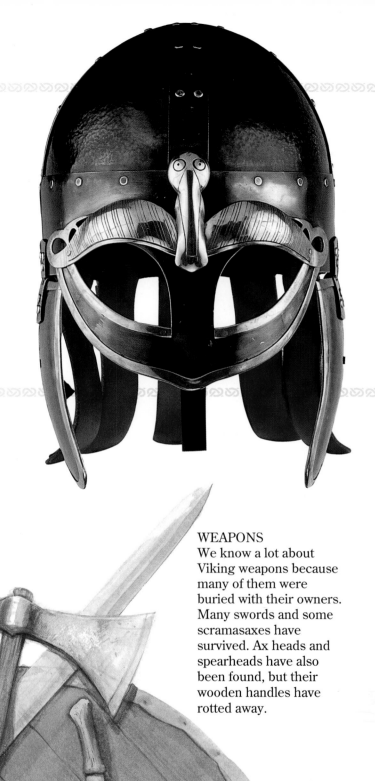

Viking warriors wore helmets to protect their heads from injury during battle. Most of them were made from thick leather, but the best ones were made of iron plates fixed onto a strong iron framework, like the one shown here. It is a reconstruction based on a helmet found on the Coppergate site in York. It is Anglo-Saxon rather than Viking, but archaeological evidence from other sites shows that Viking helmets were very similar.

THE FIGHTING LIFE

Many Vikings were warriors, as well as farmers. The early Vikings fought as individuals or for a local leader, rather than in an organized army. The warriors usually fought on foot in small groups and had to rely on surprise attack to defeat their enemies. If the enemy fought back strongly, the Vikings made a defensive wall from their wooden shields and fought as a group from behind it. Later on, the warriors started fighting for their king and became organized into armies.

Their favorite weapons were the longsword and the battle-ax, which could slice through helmets. They also used a single-edged knife called a scramasax in hand-to-hand fighting.

WEAPONS
We know a lot about Viking weapons because many of them were buried with their owners. Many swords and some scramasaxes have survived. Ax heads and spearheads have also been found, but their wooden handles have rotted away.

The earliest Viking raids took place on the coast. The Vikings would row their ships right onto the beach and launch a surprise attack.

Vast amounts of silver and gold, called Danegeld, were paid out to stop the raids on France and England. In 911 the French king solved the problem by giving Normandy to the Vikings, but the English kings kept on paying in coins.

RAIDING

When the Vikings raided a town or a monastery, they took all the treasure they could find and divided it up among themselves. They also captured as many people as they could and made them into slaves. Some of the slaves went to work for the Vikings, but many were taken to be sold in the slave markets of the Middle East.

The first raids were on coastal towns, but later the Vikings started sailing up rivers and attacking inland towns, In 845 they sailed up the Seine River and besieged Paris. They would not let anyone in or out of the city until the king agreed to pay them a large amount of silver.

This Viking ship was excavated from Oseberg, Norway, in 1904. It had been used for the burial of a royal lady in around 850 and contained everything she might need for her journey to the next life. It was buried under a mound of clay, which helped to preserve the wood. Archaeologists removed it from the ground and restored it. It contained four sledges and a wheeled cart in case the lady's journey took her over land.

TRAVEL BY SHIP

In the Viking homelands, it was easier to travel on water than on land, so ships were very important. The best known are the longships, in which the Vikings went raiding. These ships were up to 100 ft (30 m) in length. They could quickly escape from danger, as they were designed not only as sailing ships but with the additional power of being able to be rowed.

Merchant ships were shorter and broader than the longships and they carried fewer men. They had a few pairs of oars so they could move if the wind dropped, but usually they relied on their sail.

The Vikings used snowshoes to help them walk in deep snow. Sometimes they also used skis.

TRANSPORT ON LAND
The Vikings used wheeled carts on their farms. The body could be lifted off and used as a sledge if the ground was very rough. Horses were used for pulling carts and were also ridden. This beautifully carved cart is from the Oseberg ship. Those for everyday use were usually plain.

People traveling on Viking ships often got very cold and wet, although many of these ships carried tents.

VIKING ROUTES TO THE WEST
The earliest Vikings to sail west from Norway reached the Faroe and Shetland Islands. The first ones to see Iceland probably got there by accident after being blown off course in a storm. Greenland was probably discovered in the same way. In 982 Eirik the Red sailed there from Iceland and later persuaded other people to settle there. His son Leif then sailed from Greenland to reach the coast of North America and visit what is now Newfoundland.

TRAVELING TO NEW LANDS
The design of their ships was so good that the Vikings were able to sail across the North Atlantic. A few of them even visited North America. Many more took their families and farm animals to settle in Iceland and Greenland. At this time, most other Europeans hardly dared sail out of sight of land for fear of being shipwrecked. However, Viking ships were strong, but flexible. They were built up from the bottom, with the wedge-shaped planks overlapping. They were nailed to each other, then the framework was added. As this was not firmly fixed to the planks, the ship could bend slightly in rough seas instead of breaking up.

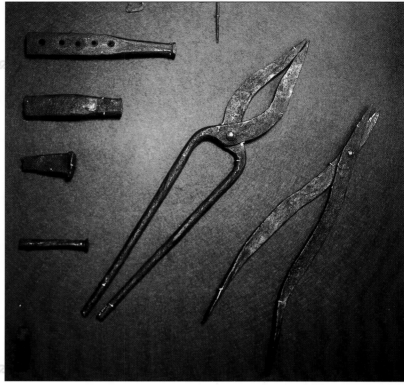

These tools from Norway belonged to a Viking blacksmith. The original wooden handles have rotted away, but the tools are very much like those still in use today. Iron ore was plentiful in the Viking lands so many farmers had a small smithy on their land to make their own tools and other iron objects. Some were helped by specialist blacksmiths who traveled from farm to farm.

CRAFTSMEN

Most Vikings lived a long way from a town. Because of this, they made most of the everyday things they needed themselves. These included clothes and furniture, as well as tools for the farm.

In bigger settlements, however, some people made a living out of making different items to sell to others. In market towns, such as Hedeby in Denmark and Birka in Sweden, we know there were Vikings who made shoes, boots, and belts from leather, swords, axes, and knives from iron, brooches and bracelets from gold, silver, and bronze, and necklaces from glass, amber, and jet beads. They also made wooden cups and bowls, pottery, and objects from bone and antler. Most of these items were sold from stalls in front of the craftsmen's houses, but some were also taken to distant farms by traveling salesmen.

TURNING A WOODEN BOWL
Wooden bowls were often made from ash or alder. The wood was cut roughly into shape and then fastened onto a pole lathe.

By pressing a treadle with his foot, the craftsman set the wood spinning around. He then held a chisel against it and hollowed the middle out as it was spinning.

He shaped the outside of the bowl in the same way, before taking it off the lathe and smoothing the top and the bottom.

To make a sword, a blacksmith heated two rods of metal in the fire then twisted them together. He then heated them again and hammered them flat to make a strong blade.

POTTERY
In England, the Vikings used pottery for jugs and storage jars, cooking pots and oil lamps, rather than for cups and plates. A pattern was sometimes made in the clay while it was still soft, and the pottery was sometimes glazed or painted.

BONE AND ANTLER
The Vikings carved pieces of bone to use as strap ends to prevent straps from fraying. They also carved buckles from bones, while antlers were cut and made into combs.

METAL
Metalworking was the most important of the Viking crafts. Iron was used for items such as nails, locks, and horseshoes, as well as for tools and weapons, while precious metals were used for jewelry and for decorating items such as drinking horns.

BUYING AND SELLING

The earliest Vikings used coins for their weight in silver rather than for any face value. Most merchants carried scales like these, which folded up into a little box. To pay for something in silver, the merchant put the correct amount in weights in one pan and balanced this with silver coins in the other pan. If the scales wouldn't balance, the merchant would cut up silver jewelry or other coins to use.

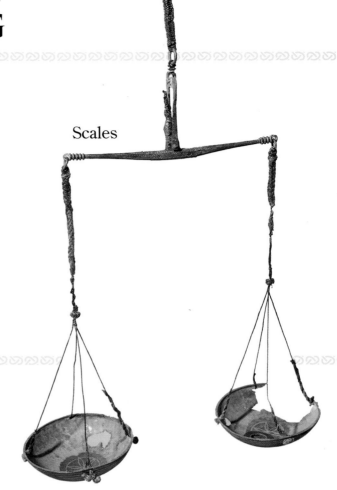

Scales

TRADING AFAR

Many Vikings made at least part of their wealth from trading. Some traveled from farm to farm, selling items made by Viking craftsmen, but others went overseas. Most traders were also farmers and they usually went trading between hay-time and the harvest. Their goods included furs, weapons, hide ropes, and soapstone bowls.

The traders took their goods off to the market towns of Birka in Sweden, Hedeby in Denmark, and Kaupang in Norway. Some also went to York in England and Dublin in Ireland. There they exchanged their goods for other things of at least equal value. They then went back home or to another market town to trade again or sell the second lot of goods at a profit.

Merchants from Iceland and Greenland, where there were no large trees, often brought cargoes of dried fish to markets in England and Norway to exchange for timber for houses and shipbuilding.

THE EVIDENCE
Some of the goods imported by Vikings have been found at Birka, Sweden. They include glass and pottery from the Rhineland, coins from Arabia and Europe, and walrus ivory from the far north.

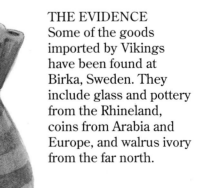

Imported goods

The city we call Istanbul was known to the Vikings as "Miklagard." There the Vikings exchanged furs, honey, beeswax, and slaves for silver, silk, brocade, and spices.

Sea routes
Overland routes
River routes

ICELAND
SHETLANDS
RUSSIA
Staraya Ladoga
Novgorod
ORKNEYS
York
Hedeby
Kiev
Istanbul

TRADE ROUTES TO THE EAST

Viking traders from Sweden crossed the Baltic to sail down the Russian rivers. Some went to Bulgar and across the Caspian Sea to reach Baghdad. Others went to Kiev and over the Black Sea to Constantinople to trade with Byzantine Greeks. In Kiev and Baghdad, they met Arab merchants who traded with the Chinese, giving the Vikings access to Chinese trade goods as well.

The main trade routes of the Vikings took them beyond the Arctic Circle and into the Mediterranean, as well as across the Atlantic and into the Black Sea. They sailed inland along river routes. In places where the rivers were difficult to sail on, they lifted their ships out of the water and carried them overland.

Rune stones can be very useful in telling us about life in Viking times. Viking warriors believed that if they died in battle they went to another life in Valhalla. This was the home of Odin, their most important god. The lower carving on this stone from Gotland in Sweden shows two of them going to Valhalla in a longship. The top carving shows one arriving there on horseback. He is being offered a drink by one of Odin's maidens.

VIKING BELIEFS

The Vikings had many different gods and goddesses. They were divided into two families, called the Aesir and Vanir. Both families lived in a place called Asgard. This was joined to earth by a rainbow bridge, called Bifrost. The earth was called Midgard. The Vikings thought it was surrounded by a deep ocean, full of monsters. Beyond this ocean was a place called Utgard, where the Frost Giants lived. They were the enemies of the gods and would eventually kill them in a battle.

The Vikings also thought that there was a place called Niflheim in the depths of the earth. It was a miserable place full of icy mists. Viking warriors believed they would be taken there in a boat made from toenail clippings if they died in bed.

Hammer

Cross

Hammer

THE COMING OF CHRISTIANITY

Traders and merchants were the first Vikings to become Christians. This made it easier for them to trade in Christian countries, but they kept to their old gods at home. As this mold shows, Viking jewelers made lucky charms in the shape of Thor's hammer, as well as making Christian crosses.

ODIN AND THOR
Odin was the god of kings, warriors, and poets. He was the most important of all the Viking gods and was very wise.

Thor was the most popular of the Viking gods. He was big and strong and had a bright red beard. He had a quick temper, but he also laughed a lot and liked to drink.

At a cremation, the body of the dead man was dressed in fine clothes and placed in a tent inside the ship. The ship was then set alight with flaming torches.

VIKING FUNERALS
Many Vikings believed that a dead person's spirit sailed to the next life in a ship. Because of this belief, some Vikings were cremated on their ships, together with all the items they needed for their journey to their new life. We know about this from Ibn Fadlan, an Arab who wrote about a Viking funeral he saw in 922. Other rich Vikings were buried in their ships under a large mound. Even poor ones often had stones set around their graves in the shape of a ship.

This wooden game board was found in Ballinderry in Ireland. This was an Irish settlement rather than a Viking one, but the board is of a Viking design. It was made in the tenth century. Nobody knows for sure what game was played on the board but perhaps it was a game called *hnefatafl*, played throughout the Viking world. This board has survived incredibly well because it was lying in a waterlogged site on the shores of a lake.

SPORTING COMPETITIONS

In their spare time, most Vikings enjoyed showing off their skills in competitive games. In the summer they enjoyed swimming and rowing races. Sometimes they held competitions to see who could walk all the way around the outside of a longship by stepping from oar to oar as it was being rowed. They also had wrestling matches, weight-lifting competitions, horse races and horse fights and gambled on who would win. In winter they made skates from the smoothed foot-bones of cattle and went skating on frozen rivers and lakes.

Children played ball games, including a kind of soccer. They are also said to have played with model boats and wooden swords. Girls probably also had wooden dolls.

FEAST TIME

Written descriptions tell us that the Vikings often wore their best clothes at feast times. They visited each other's houses and ate their food at long tables around the fire. They drank beer and mead from a drinking horn. This had to be passed around the table until it was emptied, as it could not be stood upright.

Drinking horn

THE FEASTS

Each year the Vikings had three main feasts, or holidays. Each feast could last two weeks and took the form of lots of eating, drinking, singing, dancing, and storytelling. The first was Sigrblot, which took place at the start of summer. The second was Vetrarblot, a harvest celebration. The third was Jolablot, which took place just after mid-winter.

Viking feasts were often colorful occasions. People wore bright clothes and the richest drank from silver cups.

VIKING GAMES
Vikings who traveled to the east watched the Arabs playing chess. By the eleventh century it was being played in the Viking homelands.

These Viking Age chessmen are carved out of ivory. They are part of a set which was found on the Isle of Lewis in the Hebrides.

The playing pieces that were used in Viking games were made from glass, stone, bone, wood, or ivory.

The Vikings often put up carved stones in memory of dead friends and relatives. This one is for a man called Ulf and was carved around 1020 by a man called Asmund Karesson from Osla in Uppland, Sweden. The stones are usually known as rune stones because the words on them are written in letters called runes. Many rune stones are in memory of people who died a long way from their homes.

STORIES

The Vikings were great storytellers. Families often spent the long winter evenings sitting around the fire, telling old stories and making up new ones. Not many Vikings knew how to write anything down, however. This meant that they had to learn their stories by heart and then pass them on from one generation to the next.

Many of the stories were legends, based on the adventures of the Viking gods. People liked to hear stories about Thor and his struggles with the giants who were the enemies of the gods. They also liked to hear about the lives of the Viking kings and adventurers. These stories, or sagas, were especially popular in Iceland, where many of the adventurers had lived. Most of the sagas were written down in the thirteenth century by an Icelander, called Snorri Sturluson. They were then copied many times and can still be read today.

VIKING POETRY

The Vikings enjoyed listening to poems, as well as stories. Their poets were known as *skalds*. Wealthy people often invited *skalds* to their homes when they were entertaining guests. There the *skald* would recite some of his poems and also make up new ones. Usually, one of them would be in praise of his host. His reward for this was often a valuable piece of jewelry, such as this silver bracelet.

Memorial stones were carved in the field or place where they were going to be erected, being too heavy to move around. The people who carved the runes were known as rune masters.

f	u	th	o	r
k	h	n	i	a
s	t	b	m	l	R

RUNES

As the illustration on the left shows, the Viking runes were all made up of straight lines. This made them easier to carve. There were only sixteen of them, however, and so there was not one for every sound in the language. This meant that both writing and reading the runes was very difficult, as many words had letters missing from them. Some Vikings thought the runes were magic and could protect them from danger.

ANSWERS TO MYSTERY OBJECT BOXES
Page 12: all the pieces of this object fit together into a Viking lock and key.

Page 16: this object was probably used as an ironing board. The glass object that was found with it would have been rubbed over the clothes to remove the creases.